A Look At...

Space Exploration

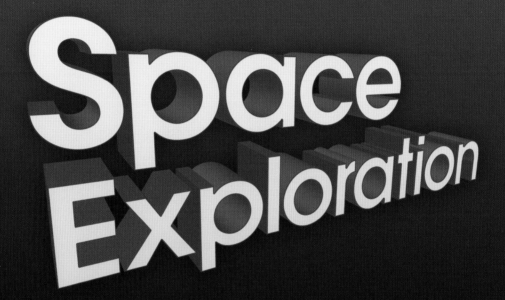

WORLD
BOOK

a Scott Fetzer company
Chicago
www.worldbookonline.com

Staff:

World Book, Inc.
233 N. Michigan Avenue
Chicago, IL 60601

For information about other World Book publications, visit our website at http://www.worldbookonline.com or call **1-800-WORLDBK (967-5325).**
For information about sales to schools and libraries, call **1-800-975-3250 (United States)**, or **1-800-837-5365 (Canada).**

Library of Congress Cataloging-in-Publication Data
Space exploration
      p. cm. -- (A look at ...)
   Includes index.
   Summary: "An introduction to space exploration, including information about the first people in space, space stations, the space shuttle, and missions to the moon, planets, and other bodies in the solar system. Features include a timeline, illustrations, photographs, a glossary, and a list of recommended books and websites."--Provided by publisher.
   ISBN 978-0-7166-1792-1
   1. Outer space--Exploration--Juvenile literature.
2. Manned space flight--Juvenile literature. I. World Book, Inc.
   QB500.262.S62 2011
   629.4'1--dc22
            2011011516

A Look At ...
Set ISBN 978-0-7166-1786-0

Printed in China by Shenzhen Donnelley Printing Co., Ltd.
Guangdong Province
1st printing July 2011

Picture Acknowledgments:

The publishers gratefully acknowledge the following sources for photography. All illustrations and maps were prepared by WORLD BOOK unless otherwise noted.

Front Cover: NASA; NASA/ESA/and M. Livio and the Hubble 20th Anniversary Team (STScI); ESA/D. Ducros

AP Photo 14, 61; Bettmann/Corbis 7, 10, 16; Roger Ressmeyer, Corbis 12; Xinhua Photos/Corbis 55; ESO/H. H. Heyer 56; Keystone/Getty Images 16; Margaret Bourke-White, Time & Life Pictures/Getty Images 40; Ralph Morse, Time Life Pictures/Getty Images 13; Esther C. Goddard 8; Iberfoto/The Image Works 7; Mary Evans Picture Library/The Image Works 6; Library of Congress 58; NASA 4, 8, 12, 13, 14, 15, 18, 19, 20, 21, 22, 23, 24, 25, 27, 28, 29, 30, 31, 32, 33, 34, 35, 37, 38, 39, 40, 42, 43, 44, 45, 49, 51, 54, 58; NASA/ESA/Hubble Heritage Team 41; NASA/ESA/M. Robberto (Space Telescope Science Institute)/Hubble Space Telescope Orion Treasury Project Team 40; NASA/ESA/UC Berkeley 48; NASA/ISAS/JAXA 57; NASA/ISS Expedition 7 Crew/EOL 4; NASA/Johns Hopkins University Applied Physics Laboratory/Carnegie Institution of Washington 46; NASA/JPL 11, 44, 45, 46, 47, 48, 50, 51, 52, 53, 57; NASA/Kepler mission/Wendy Stenzel 59; NASA/Mariner 10/Astrogeology Team/U.S. Geological Survey 46; NASA/NSSDC 43; NASA/Tony Gray & Tom Farrar 36; NASA/William K. Hartmann, UCLA 4; Mark Greenberg, New Mexico Spaceport Authority 60; Mark Garlick, Photo Researchers 52; David A. Hardy, Photo Researchers 61; RIA Novosti/Photo Researchers 18, 26; U.S. Coast Guard Navigation Center 17; U.S. Naval Research Laboratory 10, 55

CONTENTS

There is a glossary on page 62. Terms defined in the glossary are in type **that looks like this** on their first appearance on any spread (two facing pages).

Introducing Space Exploration

Space describes the vast, nearly empty regions that extend in every direction beyond Earth's atmosphere.

What is space?

We can look all around us and see things—solid things and liquid things. Even the air around us is full of such gases as oxygen. Space is quite different from this Earth on which we live.

A mixture of gases called the **atmosphere** surrounds our ball-shaped planet. Although the atmosphere is thick with gases at Earth's surface, it gets thinner the farther from Earth's surface a jet or rocket goes. At about 62 miles (100 kilometers) above Earth, the atmosphere thins out into space.

Space is the nearly empty region that stretches far beyond Earth's atmosphere. It contains far less gas and other material than any place on Earth. Without any atmosphere, space is unable to support living things. In fact, almost every living thing we know of will die almost instantly if exposed to space.

Into space

Since the mid-1950's, people have sent **satellites** and spacecraft into space. Some of the spacecraft have carried people into space. Others, called **probes,** have carried scientific instruments—but no people.

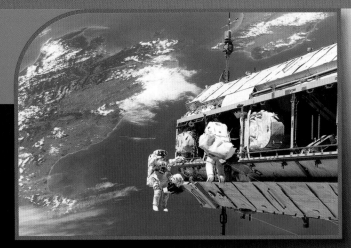

Astronauts Robert L. Curbeam, Jr. and Christer Fuglesang work to connect a new section to the International Space Station as part of NASA's STS-116 mission in 2006.

The Dawn spacecraft was built to study the two large **asteroids** Vesta, left, and Ceres, right.

Milestones of Space Travel

Date	Milestone
October 1957	Soviets launch the first satellite, Sputnik 1.
October 1959	Luna 3, a Soviet probe, photographs the moon's far side for the first time.
April 1961	Soviets send the first person, Yuri Gagarin, into space.
May 1961	The United States sends the first American, Alan Shepard, into space.
February 1962	The United States puts the first American, John Glenn, in Earth orbit.
June 1963	Soviets send the first woman, Valentina Tershkova, into space.
1964	The first successful probe to Mars, Mariner 4, transmits images.
July 1969	Astronauts of the Apollo 11 mission land on the moon.
April 1971	Soviets place Salyut 1, the first space station, in orbit.
December 1972	Astronauts walk on the moon for the final time of the century (Apollo 17).
May 1973	NASA places the first U.S. space station, Skylab, in orbit.
July 1976	The U.S. Viking probes land on Mars.
1979-1989	Voyager probes visit Jupiter, Saturn, Uranus, and Neptune.
April 1981	The United States flies its first space shuttle mission.
February 1986	Soviets place the space station Mir in orbit.
1990	NASA places the Hubble Space Telescope in orbit.
1998	Construction of the International Space Station begins.
January 2005	The Cassini-Huygens probe lands on Titan, Saturn's largest moon.
March 2009	NASA launches the Kepler probe to search for distant planets.
2011	Voyager probes approach the edge of the **solar system.**
2011	Messenger, the first satellite to orbit Mercury, transmits images.

Our bodies are not made for space

We live within Earth's protective atmosphere. Earth's gravity, the same force that pulls you to the ground, also pulls the gases in the atmosphere down. This creates air pressure, a kind of squeezing together of air particles. Human bodies are designed to live with atmospheric pressure. If a person were thrust into space without a space suit, he or she would die quickly. The absence of pressure would cause the lungs to blow out needed oxygen. Also, because of the low pressure, blood inside the body would begin to boil. That would cause the body to swell up like a balloon.

Dreams of Space Travel

Storytellers of long ago imagined travels to the moon and other heavenly bodies.

Human beings are naturally curious. In all times and places, people have asked, "What lies out there, beyond us?" Over time, the desire to travel beyond Earth became stronger.

Storytellers

People through the ages have used their imaginations to make up stories about traveling among the moon and stars. Lucian of Samosata was a Greek writer who lived about 1,850 years ago. He wrote a story in which a sailing ship travels to the moon on top of a water-spout (tornado over a body of water).

In the 1600's, an English writer, Francis Godwin, wrote a story about a voyage to the moon. Godwin imagined a spacecraft that was lifted to the moon by a flock of geese.

A more modern storyteller

Jules Verne was a French writer of the 1800's. In 1865, Verne published a book called *From the Earth to the Moon*. In Verne's story, astronauts (space explorers) traveled in a bullet-shaped metallic moonship shot from a giant cannon (tube-shaped gun that is too large to be carried by hand). Although Verne understood a great deal about the science that would be required to blast off into space, he lived a bit too early for the Space Age.

In Francis Godwin's *The Man in the Moone* (1638), a man travels to the moon on a device powered by a flock of geese.

A new way to look at the heavens

Nothing limited the imaginations of people of long ago as they stared at the heavens. But their lack of scientific knowledge meant they could do little more than dream.

Then, about 400 years ago, experts in glass-making created the first lenses for telescopes—instruments that magnify distant objects. The first scientist to study the heavens with a telescope was an Italian named Galileo. Galileo was among the first modern **astronomers,** scientists who study the heavens. (Astronomy is the science that an astronomer practices.)

Galileo's telescope

The simplest kind of telescope consists of a lens at each end of a long tube. Using a telescope like this, Galileo discovered what were later identified as the rings around the planet Saturn and two large moons on the sides of the planet.

In the years since Galileo, scientists have greatly improved telescopes. They have also made entirely different kinds of telescopes. Using these tools, scientists have learned much about the vast reaches of the heavens.

Verne's Crystal Ball

Jules Verne wrote his story of moon travel about 100 years before the first astronauts landed on the moon, but his ideas turned out to be amazingly accurate. Here are some predictions that became true.

- The United States would be the first nation to send people to the moon.

- The first moonship with astronauts would have exactly three crew members.

- This moonship would blast off from Florida.

- Upon returning to Earth, the astronauts would splash down in the Pacific Ocean. Verne's splashdown site was 123 miles (213 kilometers) from the actual location 100 years later.

Italian astronomer Galileo demonstrates his telescope to a group of observers.

Rockets

A rocket is an engine that pushes powerfully upward against the force of Earth's gravity. Rockets carry people and space exploration tools into space.

The Bumper V-2 missile launches at Cape Canaveral, Florida, on July 24, 1950. The Bumper V-2 was a two-stage rocket program used chiefly for testing rocket systems and for studying the upper **atmosphere.**

Rapid scientific progress

By the early 1900's, progress in technology helped inventors make flying machines. In 1903, Orville and Wilbur Wright flew the first airplane at Kitty Hawk, North Carolina.

Airplanes depend on the weight of air to fly. The forward movement of airplane wings through air creates lift, a force that pulls upward, against gravity.

The invention of airplanes began the age of flight. However, it did not solve the problem of how to travel in space. Airplanes need air to travel in—and there is no air in space.

The answer to this challenge was the rocket. A rocket moves by the force of a controlled explosion of fuel at one end. The burning fuel forces gases out the rear of the rocket. This action causes the rocket to move forward. Isaac Newton, an English scientist of the 1600's, explained how rockets might work. He stated the following law of motion:

For every action there is an equal and opposite reaction.

The action is the rapid escape of hot gases from the end of the rocket. The opposite reaction is the thrust, or forward movement, of the rocket. Rockets do not need wings, nor do they need air to push through. Rockets are ideal for space travel.

American rocket pioneer Robert Goddard (left) and his assistants work on an early rocket in 1940.

Rocket pioneers

The Chinese were the first people to experiment with rockets. Around the 1200's, they used small rockets in fireworks and warfare.

Around 1800, British inventor William Congreve invented small, rocket-propelled bombs to use in warfare. These rockets frightened troops but did little real damage.

The greatest advances in rockets came after 1900. Three scientists did much to advance **rocketry,** or rocket science. Konstantin Tsiolkovsky, a Russian, wrote scientific papers describing how rockets would work. Hermann Oberth, a German, and Robert Goddard, an American, tested these ideas on rockets they built.

Parts of a rocket

Rockets with the greatest lifting power are multistage rockets. These rockets have more than one stage (section). Each stage has an engine, fuel, and a supply of oxygen to help the fuel burn. When the fuel in a stage is used up, that stage drops off the rocket and falls to Earth. Many rockets also have small, powerful booster rockets, which help the spacecraft overcome gravity during the first stages of a launch.

The top part of the rocket is called the **payload.** It may include equipment for collecting data and exploring space, such as a **satellite** or **probe.** It may also include a separate capsule in which astronauts ride.

By the Rockets' Red Glare

The title above is familiar to most Americans as a phrase in "The Star-Spangled Banner," the U.S. national anthem. The "rockets' red glare" refers to British rockets fired at Ft. McHenry, near Baltimore, Maryland, during the War of 1812. These rockets were designed by British inventor William Congreve.

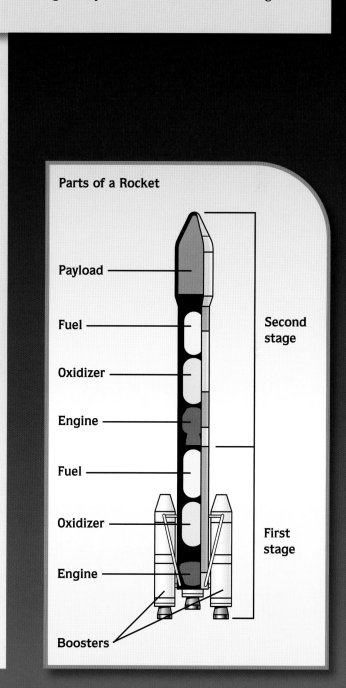

Parts of a Rocket

Payload

Fuel

Oxidizer

Engine

Fuel

Oxidizer

Engine

Boosters

Second stage

First stage

Space Age

The Space Age began in October 1957 with the launch of the artificial satellite Sputnik 1 by the Soviet Union. At the time, the Soviet Union and the United States were the two world superpowers. Competition between the two countries led to breakthroughs in space exploration.

Rockets take center stage

Work by Hermann Oberth and other German scientists led to the use of rockets in World War II (1939–1945). By the early 1940's, Germany had produced two terrifying weapons, the V-1 and the V-2. These missiles (bomb-carrying rockets) caused great destruction and loss of life in London and other English cities.

At the end of World War II, the armies of the United States and the Soviet Union occupied Germany. Both the Americans and the Soviets urged German scientists to come to their countries. After World War II, the Cold War developed between the United States and the Soviet Union. (The term *Cold War* describes the distrust and competition between the two countries.) The Americans and the Soviets started a "space race" to see who could send rockets into space first.

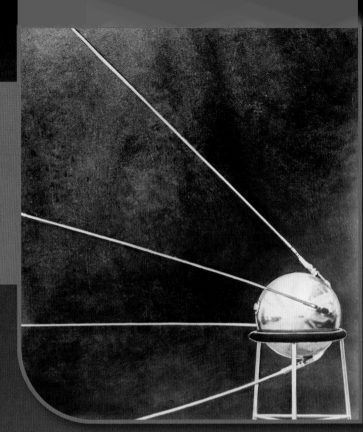

Sputnik 1, on display in a stand, circled Earth once every 96 minutes at a speed of 18,000 miles (29,000 kilometers) per hour, until it fell back to Earth on January 4, 1958.

Sputnik

The Soviets won the first phase of the space race. On October 4, 1957, they sent a **satellite** called Sputnik into orbit around Earth. (An orbit is the path of one object as it moves in a circle around another object.) Sputnik was the first human-made object to travel in an orbit around Earth. It transmitted (sent out) radio signals back to Earth so that scientists on the ground could track it.

After Sputnik 1, the Soviets sent up Sputnik 2 and 3. Meanwhile, scientists in the United States were rushing to send their first satellite into space. In December 1957, the Americans tried—and failed—to launch a satellite. In this attempt, the rocket exploded on the launchpad.

American space experts had better luck on January 31, 1958. That day, the United States successfully launched its first satellite, Explorer 1. A few weeks later, in March, the United States launched a bigger satellite called Vanguard 1.

NASA

Also in 1958, an act by the U.S. Congress created a new federal agency—the National Aeronautics and Space Administration. Today, we know it as NASA. From the beginning of the Space Age, NASA has planned and carried out almost all U.S. missions in space.

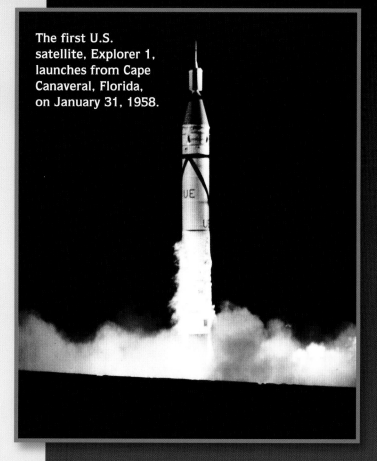

The first U.S. satellite, Explorer 1, launches from Cape Canaveral, Florida, on January 31, 1958.

A team of scientists mount the Vanguard 1 satellite in a rocket. Vanguard 1 was the second satellite launched by the United States.

At the Same Time...

During the Cold War, the Soviets and the Americans developed **rocketry** in two ways. They built rockets that could launch satellites into orbit around Earth. They also built missiles that could carry powerful nuclear bombs to far-distant places on Earth. The rockets that served as missiles did not have to push the **payload** as high as space-traveling rockets because the missiles were designed to fall back to Earth. By the mid-1900's, these powerful, long-range missiles made the Cold War more and more dangerous.

The First People in Space

In 1961, the Soviet Union became the first nation to launch a human being into space. The United States soon followed. These feats proved that people could survive in space—in the proper environment.

Cosmonaut Yuri Gagarin travels to the launchpad on April 12, 1961. Gagarin was the first person to travel into space.

Space travelers

By the early 1960's, the United States and the Soviet Union had both placed a number of **satellites** in orbit using powerful rockets. The next step was to send people into space.

This would not be an easy task. People need air to breathe, food, and water. They also must be protected from extreme heat and cold and from radiation— harmful, high-energy rays.

The Soviets tested conditions of space travel on a dog. In November 1957, they put a dog named Laika aboard Sputnik 2 and sent it into orbit on a rocket. Soviet newscasters reported that Laika did well as Sputnik 2 sped around Earth.

Another first for the Soviets

By 1961, Soviet space experts believed they were ready to put a human being into space. On April 12 of that year, the Soviets shot a rocket into space carrying 27-year-old Yuri Gagarin. Gagarin's **space capsule,** Vostok 1, circled Earth one time. Gagarin returned safely to Earth after 1 hour 48 minutes.

A Vostok capsule and SL-3 rocket are displayed in Moscow Russia. Gagarin's first flight into space was aboard the Vostok 1.

The first U.S. astronauts selected for the Mercury program. From left to right: Scott Carpenter, Gordon Cooper, John Glenn, Gus Grissom, Walter Schirra, Alan Shepard, and Donald Slayton.

Astronaut John Glenn and his wife ride with Vice President Lyndon Johnson during a 1962 parade celebrating Glenn's historic space flight.

The Americans weigh in

In the United States, a new president, John F. Kennedy, wanted the U.S. space program to catch up to the Soviet program. Seven military pilots were selected for the Mercury program, which aimed to send a human being into space. The first of this group, Alan Shepard, went into space less than a month after Yuri Gagarin's flight. Blasting off on May 5, 1961, Shepard soared to a height of 117 miles (187 kilometers) in his space capsule. Shepard did not make a complete orbit around Earth, as Gagarin had done. After 15 minutes, he returned to Earth and splashed down in the Atlantic Ocean. In July 1961, the American astronaut Gus Grissom repeated Shepard's suborbital (not making a complete orbit) flight.

An American goes into orbit

Despite Shepard's and Grissom's accomplishments, the United States still had not put an astronaut into orbit around Earth as 1961 drew to a close. That honor fell to astronaut John Glenn. He blasted off on February 20, 1962, and made three orbits of Earth. His space capsule splashed down safely in the Pacific Ocean.

People Push Farther into Space

Between 1961 and 1966, more astronauts went into space. The space travelers stayed in orbit longer and were able to do more and more tasks.

The pace quickens

In 1961 and 1962, **cosmonauts** and U.S. astronauts showed that people could go into space, survive there, and return safely to Earth. Now space experts in both countries wanted to expand their space programs. They wanted to send more people into space and have them stay in orbit for longer periods. They also wanted to give the astronauts more to do.

The Soviet Voskhod missions

In October 1964, the Soviet Union tested out a new spacecraft, Voskhod 1. This **space capsule** was capable of taking three people into orbit. The three cosmonauts on Voskhod 1 returned safely to Earth.

In March 1965, two cosmonauts blasted off in Voskhod 2. One of them, Alexei Leonov, became the first person to go on a spacewalk. Leonov entered a special tunnel called an airlock, which closed behind him. Then he was able to emerge from the tunnel into space. A cord tethered him to the spaceship as he floated high above Earth. After their exciting voyage, Leonov and his companion cosmonaut returned safely to Earth.

An external movie camera attached to the Soviet Voskhod 2 recorded Alexei Leonov's historic March 18, 1965, spacewalk—the first ever taken by a human being. **>**

First Woman in Space

In June 1963, Valentina Tereshkova, a 26-year-old Russian cosmonaut, became the first woman to travel into space. She orbited Earth 48 times in a Soviet Vostok 6 space-craft and returned to Earth safely from the history-making mission.

The name *Gemini*, from Latin, means "twin." Unlike the Mercury spacecraft, which had room for only one person, Gemini could carry two astronauts.

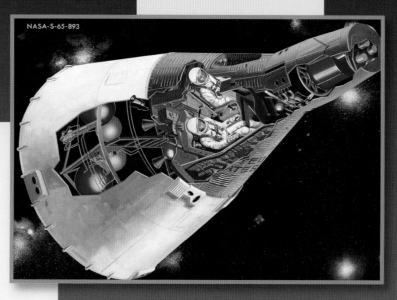

NASA-S-65-893

The U.S. Gemini missions

In 1965, the U.S. Gemini program got into full gear. Gemini spacecraft were designed to carry two astronauts. In March, Gemini 3 carried Gus Grissom and John Young into Earth's orbit. In June, Ed White became the first American to walk in space, from the Gemini 4 capsule.

The Gemini 5 mission, in August 1965, was designed to test how well astronauts would do staying in space for more than a week. Astronauts Gordon Cooper and Pete Conrad fared well during their eight days in space and returned safely to Earth.

In March 1966, U.S. astronauts aboard Gemini 8 achieved the first successful docking in space. (Docking is the act of linking two ships together so that people or things can pass between them.) They linked up with a rocket sent into space.

Gemini 12, in November 1966, was the final Gemini mission. During the mission, astronaut Buzz Aldrin spent 2½ hours repairing the outside of the spacecraft.

What's in a Name?

In Russian, *voskhod* means "sunrise." Thus, the Voskhod spacecraft was the "sunrise" ship.

Satellites

Satellites have provided many useful services since the first were rocked into orbit at the beginning of the Space Age.

The definition of *satellite* is an object that orbits Earth or some other heavenly body. By that definition, our moon is a satellite of Earth. However, when people use the word *satellite* in everyday speech, they usually mean *artificial satellite*—that is, a satellite made and placed in orbit by people. These artificial satellites perform many useful tasks.

How satellites work

A satellite is launched into space by a powerful rocket. Once the satellite is in orbit, it must keep moving at the right speed to remain in orbit. Many satellites have booster rockets that increase their speed if they begin to drift back toward Earth.

U.S. President Lyndon Johnson watches the first Eurovision Television broadcast on July 23, 1962. The broadcast was relayed by the then new communications satellite Telstar 1.

Across the Wide Ocean

In July 1962, NASA sent Telstar 1, a communications satellite, into orbit. Telstar 1 allowed U.S. broadcasters to send television broadcasts from the United States to France in real time. The first such "live" broadcast took place on July 10, the day Telstar was launched. This marked the first time that people in North America and Europe could simultaneously view events from across the Atlantic Ocean as they were happening.

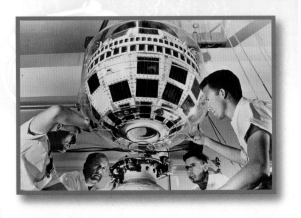

Communications satellites

From the days of Sputnik, scientists realized that satellites could receive and transmit message-carrying radio signals. Satellite transmission would have a huge advantage. When a radio signal is sent out from ground level, its waves of energy travel in straight lines. This means that a receiver far around Earth's curve is unable to receive that signal. However, by bouncing signals off orbiting satellites, radio signals could be sent and received all around the world. Today, these signals carry telephone calls, television programs, Internet traffic, and other information.

The United States launched its first modern communications satellite, Echo 1, in August 1960. Today, there are many communications satellites in orbit.

Navigation satellites

Navigation means "finding one's route or way." Navigation satellites provide services that help people identify their location or find their way. Many navigation services are based on the Global Positioning System (GPS). GPS allows people to determine exactly where they are on Earth. The GPS system relies on more than 20 satellites working together.

Weather satellites

Weather forecasting has improved greatly since the start of the Space Age. In part, this is because weather satellites take pictures of cloud patterns and collect data about the **atmosphere.** Forecasters use these data to make their predictions.

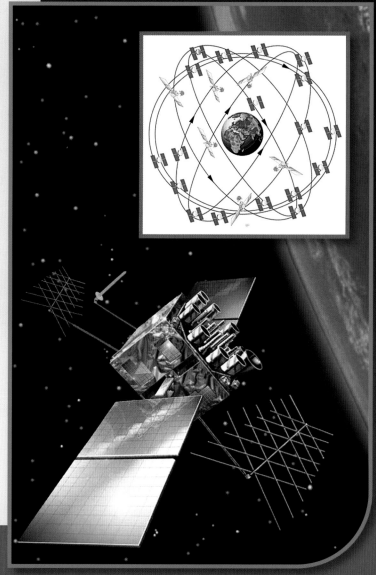

GPS satellites orbit Earth, broadcasting radio signals. Receivers in aircraft, surface vehicles, and handheld units can use these signals to determine location.

Destination: Moon

The moon has always fascinated human beings. From the beginning of the Space Age, scientists made plans to travel to Earth's nearest neighbor.

A close neighbor

The moon is on average only 239,000 miles (385,000 kilometers) from Earth—about 35 times the distance between New York City and Beijing. Venus, our nearest neighbor among the planets, never comes any closer to Earth than 23.7 million miles (38.2 million kilometers). That's almost 100 times the distance between Earth and the moon. When people began thinking about sending spaceships from Earth to a distant heavenly body, the moon was the obvious choice.

The moon is Earth's natural **satellite.** Like any satellite, it travels in an orbit. It orbits Earth once every 29½ days.

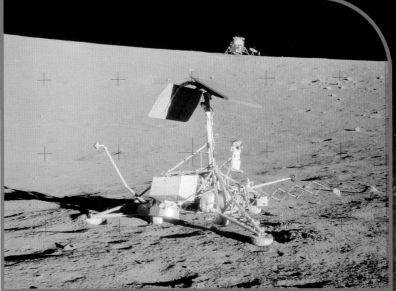

The U.S. Surveyor 3 spacecraft on the lunar surface. The Surveyor program made a series of successful soft lunar landings beginning in 1966.

The moon and the Space Age

After the Soviet Union launched Sputnik in 1957, Soviet scientists began to work feverishly to send **probes** to the moon. In January 1959, the Soviets launched their first moon probe. Luna 1, as it was called, traveled to the moon, took scientific measurements as it passed within several thousand miles, and then zoomed out into space. This was the first data about the moon that scientists on Earth received from a moon probe. In September and October 1959, the Soviets launched Luna 2 and Luna 3.

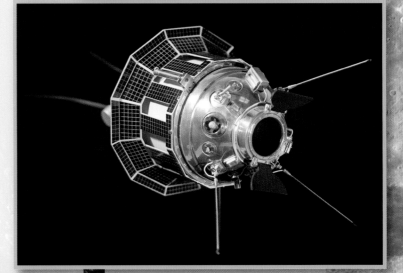

In 1959, the Luna 3 spacecraft photographed the far side of the moon, which cannot be seen from Earth.

More Luna missions

The Soviets resumed their highly successful Luna program in 1963. Between 1963 and 1976, the Soviets carried out 21 Luna missions. One of the most important was Luna 9 in January 1966.

Luna 9 landed safely on the moon's surface and sent back television pictures—the first ground-level views of the moon. The mission convinced scientists that a spacecraft could be landed safely and that astronauts could, someday, walk on the moon.

U.S. moon probes

NASA sponsored two moon exploration programs before sending astronauts to the moon. In 1964 and 1965, several Ranger probes returned thousands of pictures from their flybys (orbits around the moon). In 1966 and 1967, seven Surveyor probes explored the moon. Five of these probes touched down successfully on the moon's surface. These accomplishments provided much scientific knowledge. They also gave NASA scientists confidence that they could plan a mission to land astronauts on the moon.

A bold prediction

In May 1961, President John F. Kennedy declared that the United States would send astronauts to the moon by the end of the 1960's. The challenge seemed impossible. The United States and the Soviet Union were just beginning to send people into space in 1961. Only time would tell whether Kennedy's bold prediction would prove true.

U.S. President John F. Kennedy launched a race to the moon with a historic speech

The Apollo Program

The Apollo program successfully took U.S. astronauts to the moon on a series of missions.

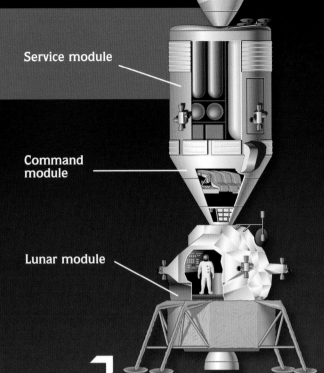

Service module

Command module

Lunar module

The Apollo spacecraft carried three astronauts in its command module into orbit around the moon.

The Apollo spacecraft

In the mid-1960's, NASA developed the Apollo spacecraft. Based on an entirely new design, Apollo would carry three astronauts to the moon. It would allow two astronauts to descend to the moon's surface in a smaller spaceship. After a brief visit to the moon, these two astronauts would fly back to the main spacecraft.

The Apollo spacecraft consisted of three parts. The command module (CM) was the main cabin in which the astronauts would live and work. (A **module** is a section that can function either by itself or with other parts.) The service module (SM) contained supplies, fuel, and the main rocket engine. The lunar module (LM) was the small spaceship that would take astronauts to and from the moon's surface. (*Lunar* means "of the moon.")

Tragedy on the launchpad

On January 27, 1967, astronauts Gus Grissom, Ed White, and Roger Chaffee were inside the command module of Apollo 1 atop its rocket on the launchpad at Cape Canaveral, Florida. The actual launch was weeks away, but they were receiving Apollo training.

Suddenly, a spark started a fire and burned fiercely. All three astronauts were killed. The accident was the first great tragedy of America's space program.

The crew of the planned first piloted U.S. Apollo space flight—Gus Grissom, Ed White, and Roger Chaffee—were killed in a tragic accident at Cape Canaveral on January 27, 1967.

Apollo 7 astronauts Walter Schirra and Donn Eisele are seen in the first live television transmission from space on October 14, 1968.

Getting back on track

After the tragedy of January 1967, NASA postponed upcoming missions. **Engineers** went back to work on the Apollo spacecraft, and NASA conducted several unpiloted Apollo missions. Only after 1½ years did NASA give the go-ahead for a piloted Apollo flight.

On October 11, 1968, a giant rocket blasted off from the Cape Canaveral launchpad carrying three astronauts. The mission, Apollo 7, orbited Earth for four days.

The next mission, Apollo 8, blasted off on December 21 with a three-man crew. Apollo 8 headed straight for the moon. As it neared the moon three days later, the spacecraft went into lunar orbit. Apollo 8 did not land on the moon. But the orbit was the closest people had ever been to the moon. On December 24, 1968, the Apollo 8 astronauts broadcast television images to Earth.

More Apollo missions

In early 1969, NASA launched two more moon missions. Apollo 9 and 10 astronauts tested the spacecraft in a number of ways without actually landing.

What's in a Name?

The Apollo mission was named for the Greek God Apollo, whom the ancient Greeks thought to be a giver of light, music, poetry, and the arts.

Tragedy for the Soviets

The Soviet space program also suffered tragedy in 1967. Vladimir Komarov was the first **cosmonaut** to fly in Soyuz 1, a new spacecraft. He died on April 24 when the craft's parachute failed to open as Soyuz 1 fell to Earth.

In July 1969, the United States successfully landed the first astronauts on the moon.

Around the middle of 1969, NASA officials decided it was time to land human beings on the moon. The successes of Apollo 7, 8, 9, and 10 had convinced them that the Apollo spacecraft, including the all-important lunar **module,** would perform as expected.

Apollo 11

NASA planned the Apollo 11 mission for July and chose three astronauts: Neil Armstrong, Michael Collins, and Buzz Aldrin. From moon orbit, Armstrong and Aldrin were to board the lunar module and descend to the surface of the moon. Collins would remain with the command module.

Eight days in history

In the Apollo 11 spacecraft atop a Saturn 5 rocket, Armstrong, Aldrin, and Collins blasted off on July 16, 1969. Entering the moon's orbit on July 19, the Apollo 11 astronauts held the world's attention.

On July 20, Aldrin and Armstrong strapped themselves into Eagle—the lunar module. Eagle detached from the command module—Columbia—and began its descent to the lunar surface. Minutes later, Eagle touched down amid a cloud of dust kicked up by its engine. People were on the moon!

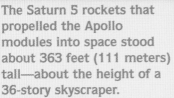

The Saturn 5 rockets that propelled the Apollo modules into space stood about 363 feet (111 meters) tall—about the height of a 36-story skyscraper.

Into the unknown

It was time for human beings to step into a new world. Neil Armstrong turned on a television camera, opened the hatch (door), and walked down a ladder. As he planted his left foot on solid moonground, Armstrong said, "That's one small step for a man, one giant leap for mankind." Armstrong's "small step" on the moon was something people had dreamed about for thousands of years.

What they found

Aldrin soon joined Armstrong outside the space-craft. The astronauts reported that the top layer of moonsoil was a fine gray powder. They saw many craters and boulders scattered about. The sky was pitch black because there was no **atmosphere** to scatter light. Aldrin and Armstrong made their way carefully because the moon's weak gravity made them feel lightweight. They collected samples of moon rocks for scientific study on Earth.

According to plan

Returning to the Eagle, Aldrin and Armstrong fired its rockets. They took off and steered the Eagle back to Columbia, orbiting above the moon. After Aldrin and Armstrong were safely aboard, Columbia headed for Earth. The astronauts splashed down in the Pacific Ocean on July 24. The mission had gone off perfectly.

Buzz Aldrin stands next to the U.S. flag he had planted on the lunar surface. Neil Armstrong took the picture on July 20, 1969.

Apollo 11 crew. From left to right: Neil Armstrong, Michael Collins, and Buzz Aldrin.

More Moon Missions

NASA followed up the success of Apollo 11 with five more moon missions. The final mission, Apollo 17 in 1972, marked the end of the first chapter of human moon exploration.

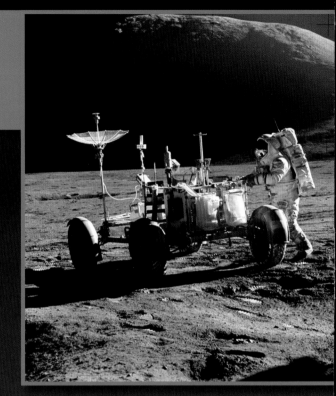

Apollo 12

The spectacular Apollo 11 mission was just the beginning of human exploration of the moon. In November 1969, Apollo 12 headed for the moon with three different astronauts. Apollo 12 landed on a different part of the moon. The Apollo 12 astronauts returned safely to Earth, with more moon rocks and some parts of the old Surveyor **probe.**

Apollo 13

NASA was soon ready for another moon mission. In April 1970, astronauts Jim Lovell, Jack Swigert, and Fred Haise blasted off for the moon. Two days after liftoff, the astronauts heard a bang in the service **module** next to their cabin. An explosion had disabled the service module. That meant that the astronauts had very little air, water, fuel, and other supplies.

The astronauts—and their NASA support team at Mission Control Center in Houston— realized that the three men had only a slim chance for survival. The Control Center went to overdrive and managed to bring Lovell, Swigert, and Haise safely home. They splashed down in the Pacific Ocean on April 17.

After the troubles with Apollo 13, NASA brought the Apollo program to a halt. Scientists and **engineers** studied the data from the mission. They found the cause of the explosion in the service module and fixed it.

Flight controllers from Mission Control in Houston watch the splashdown of Apollo 13 on April 17, 1970. Against all odds, the Control Center had managed to bring the astronauts home after an explosion left them with little air, water, or fuel. ⌄

At a top speed of 6 miles (10 kilometers) per hour, the lunar rover was not a speed demon. But it allowed the astronauts to explore more of the moon than ever before.

The next four Apollo missions

NASA resumed Apollo flights in February 1971 with Apollo 14. Alan Shepard commanded the mission. In 1961, Shepard had been the first American to travel into space. Unlike Apollo 13, Apollo 14 had been a nearly perfect mission.

Apollo 15 traveled to the moon in July 1971. This time, the astronauts in the lunar module had a special companion—the lunar **rover** (a battery-powered four-wheeled vehicle that carries scientific instruments). They landed on the moon, rolled out the rover, and explored in all directions.

Apollo 16 took place in April 1972. The astronauts explored more of the lunar surface. Like Apollo 15 before, Apollo 16 was a great success.

The final Apollo mission, Apollo 17, took place in December 1972. During a moonwalk, astronaut Harrison Schmitt made a surprising discovery. He found some orange-colored soil to take back to NASA labs. Before lifting off from the moon, astronaut Eugene Cernan said, "…We leave as we came and, God willing, as we shall return, with peace and hope for all mankind." As it turned out, no human being walked on the moon for the rest of the century.

Crew members of the Apollo 13 mission step aboard a recovery ship after landing in the South Pacific Ocean. From left to right, Fred Haise, Jim Lovell, and Jack Swigert.

Space Stations

In the 1960's, the Soviet Union and the United States developed the first space stations—orbiting satellites that have enough room for several astronauts to live and work for long periods.

Between the early 1960's and the early 1970's, both the Soviet Union and the United States sent dozens of astronauts into space. None of these astronauts could stay in space for very long, however. Their spacecraft carried them to a destination and then right back to Earth.

Scientists, national leaders, and many citizens wanted people to live in space for longer periods in anticipation of long journeys in the **solar system** (the sun, its planets, and all other bodies that orbit the sun). The space station was the most practical way to accomplish this. Like **satellites**, space stations would need to be designed to orbit above Earth's **atmosphere** and for years at a time.

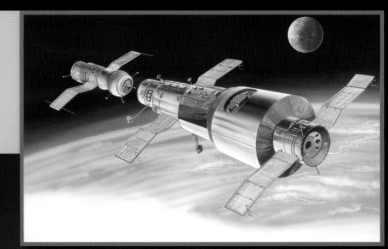

▲ In an artist's rendering, a Soviet Soyuz spacecraft docks with the Salyut space station in orbit above Earth.

Soyuz 11 crew members (from left to right) Viktor Patsayev, Georgi Dobrovolski, and Vladislav Volkov smile before take-off on June 6, 1971.

Why space stations?

After 10 years of human space flights, space scientists on Earth still did not know much about how human bodies react to conditions in space. One of the most challenging, **microgravity,** is the condition of having so little gravity that a human body is almost weightless. Doctors were eager to study astronauts living in the conditions of microgravity on space stations.

Many other space scientists wanted to study conditions in space. Some were interested in learning how crops grow in space. Others wanted to find out if certain ways of making products would be easier in microgravity than on Earth. Such people imagined factories humming on space stations far above Earth.

The work begins

By the early 1970's, space officials in both the Soviet Union and the United States were focusing on space stations. Putting space stations in orbit and sending astronauts to and from them would be the next big challenge.

Another first for the Soviets

In 1971, Soviets put the world's first space station, Salyut 1, in orbit. Shaped like a round can, Salyut had room for three astronauts to live and work in space. Sticking out from the "can" were **solar panels.** A solar panel is a flat, thin surface that contains thousands of solar cells. These tiny devices change the energy from sunlight into electricity.

In June 1971, three **cosmonauts** arrived at Salyut in the Soyuz 11 spacecraft. They docked and went aboard the space station. The cosmonauts stayed at the station for 24 days. Then they re-entered their Soyuz spacecraft and returned to Earth. Tragically, the astronauts died on June 29 just before reaching ground. A leak in the spacecraft sucked out all of their air.

Astronaut Christer Fuglesang trains in NASA's Neutral Buoyancy Laboratory, which imitates the microgravity conditions of space.

NASA put the first U.S. space station, Skylab, into orbit in 1973. The Soviet space station Mir was launched in 1986.

A U.S. space station

Like the Soviet space agency, NASA was also developing a space station in the early 1970's. In May 1973, a Saturn 5 rocket blasted off from Florida, propelling Skylab into orbit.

Skylab had a shaky start. Shortly after liftoff, a sheet of metal on the side of the space station ripped away. This accident tore off one of Skylab's four **solar panels** and damaged a second one.

Repair work begins

Ten days after Skylab's launch, three astronauts aboard an Apollo spacecraft headed toward Skylab with a toolkit, ready to make repairs. After hard, dangerous work on the outside of Skylab, the astronauts repaired the damaged solar panel. They remained aboard for 28 days.

More crews arrive

In 1973 and early 1974, two more three-person crews boarded Skylab. The final crew lived and worked on Skylab for about three months.

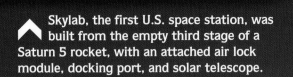

Skylab, the first U.S. space station, was built from the empty third stage of a Saturn 5 rocket, with an attached air lock module, docking port, and solar telescope.

A Saturn 5 rocket launches Skylab into orbit on May 14, 1973. An accident shortly after liftoff tore off one of Skylab's four solar panels and damaged a second one.

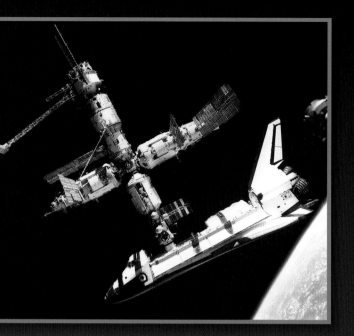

The space shuttle Atlantis docks with the Russian Mir space station in July 1995. The shuttle transported a replacement crew of cosmonauts to Mir and brought the station's former crew home to Earth.

In Lockstep

Skylab had a special arrangement to help keep astronauts from floating about. The floors, instead of being solid, were made of a metal grid (crisscross pattern). An astronaut matched up a cleat (piece that sticks out) on his shoe sole with a shape in the grid—and then locked it in place by turning the shoe.

Scientific accomplishments

Skylab had a special **module** containing six telescopes for studying the sun. These telescopes captured views of the sun never before seen. Photographs from the telescopes demonstrated as never before the advantages of studying the heavens from space.

Skylab astronauts also conducted many scientific experiments. One such experiment revealed that in space, spiders spun highly irregular webs!

Mir space station

In February 1986, the Soviet Union launched its new space station, Mir. Soviet **engineers** designed Mir as a series of modules that could be sent into orbit one at a time and linked up in space. Between 1986 and 1996, five modules were added to the original core.

The Mir modules included laboratories to study Earth from space and outer space from outside Earth's **atmosphere.** Other modules were storage units. One was a docking bay to receive or launch **satellites** and other vehicles.

An international team

In all, 105 astronauts lived and worked on Mir at one time or another. Mir was truly international. Astronauts from Austria, France, Germany, the United States, and other countries spent time on Mir.

One **cosmonaut,** Valery Polyakov, spent 438 days on Mir. His stay on the space station proved that people could live and work in space for long periods.

Mir itself set a new record for time in space. It lasted from 1986 until 2001, when it was allowed to drop out of orbit and burn up in Earth's atmosphere.

The International Space Station

In 1998, astronauts of various nations began to assemble the International Space Station in Earth's orbit. It became an important laboratory for research in space.

The International Space Station functions as an observatory, laboratory, and workshop. **Solar panels** furnish the electric power for the station.

In the 1990's, the space agencies of several countries decided to work together to build and run a new space station. It would be called the International Space Station (ISS).

The United States and Russia (formerly the Soviet Union) cooperated as allies in the ISS project. They were joined by the European Space Agency (ESA). The ESA, the space agency of the European Union, was growing in importance. Brazil, Canada, and some other nations participated as well.

Like Mir, the ISS was designed as a string of **modules** that could be linked together in space. The first module was placed in orbit in 1998. Others were soon added. The station could support three-member crews. The first full-time crew arrived at the ISS in November 2000.

Recent upgrades

In 2009, the electric power system and the water system of the ISS were expanded. After that, six crew members could stay on the station for long periods.

The station was originally designed to last only until 2015. However, the space agencies decided to keep it in good running order until at least 2020.

Astronauts Pam Melroy, Peggy Whitson, and Stephanie Wilson aboard the International Space Station in 2007. ⌄

ISS Firsts

- First space station to contain parts made in different nations.

- Most astronauts in orbit together at one time.

- Longest occupied space station.

- First space tourist: American Dennis Tito in 2001, who paid his own way.

- First South African in space: Mark Shuttleworth, a space tourist, in 2002.

- First Brazilian in space: Marcos Cesar Pontes in 2006.

- First Korean in space: Yi So-yeon in 2008.

- First woman commander: American Peggy Whitson, between October 2007 and April 2008.

- First space robot for performing repairs on the outside of a space station: "Dextre," the robot, became fully functional in 2010.

- First toy astronaut assigned to the ISS: NASA sent Buzz Lightyear to the ISS in 2008 as part of an education program for young people. Buzz returned to Earth on September 11, 2009.

Science Studies Aboard the ISS

- Studies of Earth's polar regions from space have helped scientists better understand climate change. Over the past 100 years or more, Earth has been warming, and the polar regions are heating up faster than the rest of the planet.

- Study in space of proteins and other complex molecules revealed that the thousands of parts of these molecules spread farther apart in **microgravity**. They can, therefore, be studied more easily in space. Study of proteins aboard the ISS has helped drug companies on Earth develop new treatments.

- Scientists aboard the ISS have conducted groundbreaking studies of plasma, a form of matter composed of electrically charged particles.

Mark Shuttleworth, shown aboard the International Space Station, became the first South African to travel into space in 2002.

Living and Working in Space

Scientists and engineers have had to work hard to create conditions on space stations similar to those on Earth.

People living in space have the same needs as those living on Earth. Such space stations as the ISS are designed to meet all of these needs.

The breath of life

Earth's **atmosphere** consists of oxygen and nitrogen, with some other gases mixed in. This rich mix of air must be provided inside space stations, and it must be at the right temperature and the right pressure to sustain life.

Ventilation (airflow) systems on space stations are designed to duplicate atmospheric conditions on Earth. To accomplish this, a station must keep canisters of compressed oxygen and nitrogen in storage. The ventilation system must have filters to keep the air clean and instruments to test the air continually.

Eating and drinking in space

Food and water must be carried to the space station on spacecraft and stored onboard. To cook food on the ISS, astronauts use a specially designed oven. The oven shoots jets of very hot air at the food. It cooks the food directly without heating the surroundings.

Eating and drinking in the **microgravity** of space orbit present challenges. Food and liquid tend to rise out of containers and float around the room. Space **engineers** design special plates, bowls, and glasses that keep food and drink in place.

▲ Astronaut Peggy Whitson sits in a sleeping compartment aboard the International Space Station.

Packaged food floats aboard the Russian Zvezda service **module.** ▼

Using the bathroom

Microgravity presents challenges for using the bathroom, too. On the ISS, astronauts use a specially designed toilet. It uses air suction to pull the waste material into the station's waste treatment center.

Taking a shower

Think about taking a shower. The water falls from the showerhead, strikes your body, runs off it, and then goes down the drain. In space, there is no gravity to make the water run down. Showers on the ISS are designed with suction to pull the dirty water into containers from where they can be channeled back into the water treatment system.

Sleeping

Astronauts use special sleeping bags in space. These bags have straps that hold an astronaut's sleeping body in place. Some astronauts prefer to sleep floating in air. They can do this safely by attaching themselves to the wall with special straps.

Exercise and recreation

Physical activity is extremely important for astronauts living on a space station. Because of microgravity, people's muscles have almost no work to do. This causes them to become weak. Astronauts keep their muscles fit with regular daily exercise on stationary bikes and other exercise machines.

Astronauts also need to have fun sometimes if they are to enjoy good mental health. Astronauts generally make their own fun. They also have books, music players, and electronic games.

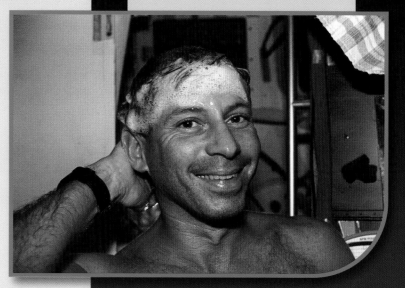

Astronaut Ken Cockrell washes his hair aboard the space shuttle Columbia. Astronauts in space use a special shampoo that does not need to be rinsed out.

Tortillas in Space

NASA astronaut Sandra Magnus discovered an easy way to make mealtime more appealing on the ISS. She used tortillas as much as possible. Magnus noted that many foods can be served on or inside a tortilla—taco style. She put in big orders to NASA for tortillas. Magnus lived on the ISS between November 2008 and March 2009.

Today, medical researchers study the ways in which conditions in space affect the human body, and doctors are learning to treat these conditions.

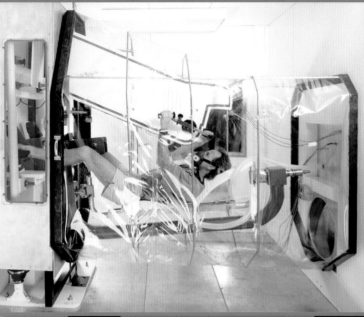

On Earth, human muscles, bones, and the circulatory system (the heart and all the blood vessels that carry blood throughout the body) work efficiently against the force of Earth's gravity. In space, conditions are different, and the body has to adjust.

Muscles and bones

In space, muscles and bones do not have to work hard. They are not constantly pulling against gravity, as on Earth. Muscles that don't have to work soon become weak and slack. In time, they become thinner. Also, bones loose calcium and become weaker.

To prevent serious harm to muscles and bones, astronauts exercise for several hours each day. They also eat foods with vitamins and minerals that help bones grow.

Heart and blood

The heart is the powerful muscle that pumps blood through the body. In space, because of **microgravity,** the heart doesn't have to pump as hard. This causes the heart to become weaker. Under these conditions, the body makes less blood, so the total amount of blood inside the body decreases.

Space **engineers** are working to create special chambers with artificial gravity. Astronauts will be able to exercise inside these chambers to strengthen their heart, blood vessels, muscles, and bones.

An astronaut trains on the Standalone Zero Gravity Locomotion Simulator (sZLS), which imitates what it is like to exercise in weightlessness. The sZLS was developed to improve exercise routines for astronauts during spaceflight.

Long-Distance Medicine

Medical treatment of astronauts aboard the ISS has led to new techniques described as telemedicine. Telemedicine allows doctors to examine and treat a person without being present. Television pictures and other data about a patient can be sent to a doctor at mission control back on Earth.

The need to treat sick astronauts in space is spurring special medical research on Earth. For example, space engineers have developed hand-held machines that can perform scans of body parts. The machines use ultrasound—sound waves with such a high pitch that people can't hear them.

Telemedicine is helping astronauts stay healthy in space. It is also becoming a useful tool for treating sick people in faraway places here on Earth.

International Space Station Commander Leroy Chiao performs an ultrasound examination of the eye on astronaut Salizhan Sharipov. Space engineers developed such hand-held machines to perform scans of body parts that can be relayed to a doctor on Earth.

Sense of balance

There is no rightside-up or upside-down in space. However, our brains are programmed to sense "up" and "down." When the brain can't pick up these signals, motion sickness may result. Astronauts with motion sickness feel dizzy and nauseous. They may even throw up. In time, the motion sickness passes.

The immune system

Doctors have discovered that the body's immune system doesn't work as well in space as on Earth. White blood cells called killer T-cells are important parts of the immune system. When doctors study astronauts' T-cells, they detect unusual changes.

T-cells typically have a very uneven shape. The wavy surface of these cells helps them surround germs and digest them.

But in space, astronauts' T-cells become rounder and smoother. They can't surround germs as easily. Researchers suspect that this change is caused by microgravity. Because of lowered immunity, it's important for astronauts to stay clean and to keep supplies of antibiotics on hand to fight infections.

A new kind of spacecraft, the space shuttle, began flying missions in 1981.

Growing pains

The spacecraft of the 1960's and 1970's carried people into orbit around Earth and to the moon. However, NASA **engineers** realized that a different type of spacecraft would be needed in the era of space stations.

The Apollo- and Soyuz-type vehicles had serious drawbacks. They were too small to carry much cargo. And they were designed to be used only once. These factors meant that going back and forth between Earth and space stations was extremely costly.

A new kind of spaceship

To meet these challenges, NASA scientists and engineers designed the space shuttle. This spacecraft "shuttled"—went back and forth—between Earth and orbiting space stations.

The space shuttle was like a bulky jet plane. Rockets boosted it into orbit like other spacecraft. But the shuttle could fly back to Earth and land on a runway just like a jet, and it was used over and over again. The shuttle could carry eight passengers and such cargo as communications **satellites** or **modules** of the International Space Station.

First voyage

U.S. astronauts John Young and Robert Crippen flew the first shuttle mission in the space shuttle Columbia in April 1981. At the end of the five-day flight, they landed smoothly on the runway at Edwards Air Force Base in California.

The space shuttle Atlantis at liftoff. Atlantis completed a series of missions in the 1990's and early 2000's.

The U.S. Space Shuttles

Name	Date of First Flight
Enterprise	1977*
Columbia	1981
Challenger	1983
Discovery	1984
Atlantis	1985
Endeavour	1992

*Flight tests only

More missions, more shuttles

NASA was thinking big. Even as Columbia aced its first shuttle mission in April 1981, the space agency was building other shuttles. The shuttle Challenger made its first voyage in April 1983. In all, NASA built six U.S. space shuttles, and five were sent into space.

The Ace Moving Company

NASA planned for its shuttles to haul satellites and other hardware into space for communications companies and other companies. NASA would charge for these services and recover some of the cost of building the shuttles. In November 1982, astronauts aboard Columbia called themselves the "Ace Moving Company." The astronauts were having some fun, but their joke pointed out an important part of the shuttle missions. Since 1982, space shuttles have placed dozens of satellites in orbit.

Shuttle astronauts also repaired broken satellites in orbit. This was another way for NASA to make money from communications companies on Earth.

The space shuttle Discovery in orbit above Earth.

The space shuttle Endeavour lands at Edwards Air Force Base in California on October 11, 1994. A drag chute attached to the spacecraft helps to slow the vehicle at landing.

The shuttle program was successful in many ways. It suffered some terrible tragedies, too.

The Challenger disaster

January 28, 1986, was supposed to be a day of celebration. People across the United States anxiously awaited the launch of the Challenger shuttle. Among the shuttle's seven crew members was Christa McAuliffe, who had been chosen to be the first school teacher to travel in space. As people around the world watched, the Challenger broke apart only 73 seconds after liftoff. All of the crew members were killed.

After the Challenger disaster, NASA postponed all upcoming shuttle flights. **Engineers** found the cause of the accident—a tiny defective part.

Back in the saddle

The shuttle program started up again in September 1988. That month, the Discovery flew a mission to place a **satellite** in orbit.

The space shuttle became an important supply line to space stations—first to Mir and then to the ISS. Shuttles ferried crews back and forth between the stations and Earth. They also brought fresh supplies to the people living and working on space stations.

The space shuttle Challenger disaster occurred just over a minute after launch on January 28, 1986.

The Challenger crew members. Back row, left to right: Ellison Onizuka, Christa McAuliffe, Greg Jarvis, and Judy Resnik. Front row, left to right: Mike Smith, Dick Scobee, and Ron McNair.

The Columbia disaster

On February 1, 2003, the space shuttle Columbia broke up over the southwestern United States on its descent to land in Florida. The disaster took the lives of all seven astronauts aboard. NASA postponed all upcoming shuttle missions. Investigators found that a chunk of foam insulation had broken off during liftoff and damaged one of the shuttle's wings. However, no one knew at the time that the wing had been damaged.

The Columbia crew members. From left to right: David Brown, Rick Husband, Laurel Clark, Kalpana Chawla, Michael Anderson, William McCool, and Ilan Ramon.

Recent shuttle missions

By July 2005, NASA was again ready to launch shuttle missions. On July 26, Discovery blasted off into space after almost 2½ years of shuttle inactivity.

Between 2005 and 2011, shuttles hauled a number of **modules** to the ISS. The shuttle program played a major part in assembling the space station. In fact, the ISS would probably not have been possible without the U.S. shuttle fleet.

Farewell

Like all human-made machines, the shuttle fleet has aged over time. Engineers designed the shuttles knowing that, some day, they would outlive their usefulness. After several flights in 2011, the last shuttle was retired in June 2011. NASA engineers have developed a new spacecraft that will carry astronauts to the ISS, the moon, and beyond. Its name is Orion.

An Ill-Fated First

One of the crew members who died in the Columbia disaster of February 2003 was Ilan Ramon. He was the first Israeli to travel in space.

The Hubble Space Telescope

In 1990, NASA put the Hubble Space Telescope into orbit around Earth. Astronomers have used the powerful telescope to obtain images of celestial objects and events in detail never before observed.

Edwin Hubble peers through the eyepiece of a telescope in 1937. Hubble was a renowned astronomer for whom the Hubble Space Telescope was named.

Seeing in space

All Earth-based telescopes view the heavens through Earth's **atmosphere.** This thick layer of gases, usually in motion, blurs the images we see. However, images of distant heavenly bodies viewed from space are not distorted by the effects of Earth's atmosphere. For these reasons, NASA and other space agencies made plans to build and launch space telescopes.

In 1990, the space shuttle Discovery placed the Hubble Space Telescope in orbit 380 miles (610 kilometers) above Earth. However, a 94-inch (239-centimeter) mirror in the telescope had a flaw that made the images blurry. In December 1993, NASA sent a crew aboard the space shuttle Endeavour to repair Hubble. The astronauts installed two new parts that corrected the mirror's flaw.

How it works

The Hubble responds to instructions sent by scientists on Earth. These instructions are in the form of radio signals. Hubble codes the pictures it takes as radio signals and sends the signals back to Earth.

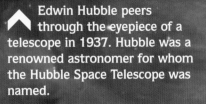

An image of the Hubble Space Telescope taken from the space shuttle Atlantis in May 2009.

What's in a Name?

The Hubble Space Telescope is named for American **astronomer** Edwin P. Hubble (1889–1953). Hubble discovered galaxies beyond our own. He realized that vast parts of the universe lay beyond our own galaxy, the Milky Way.

Astonishing images

The Hubble telescope has taken thousands of pictures of incredible clarity and beauty. Many of its images have been of distant stars or galaxies never viewed before. (A **galaxy** is a vast system of stars, gas, dust, and other matter held together in space by their mutual gravitational pull.)

Following the important 1993 repair mission, NASA made plans to send astronauts to the telescope on a regular basis. In 2009, NASA sent its final servicing mission to the Hubble. NASA officials expect the Hubble telescope to keep working well until at least 2014. Meanwhile, NASA plans to launch a new telescope, the James Webb Space Telescope, soon after Hubble is retired.

Massive columns of dust and gas light-years long project from a nebula (cloudlike cluster of stars). The columns are called "the pillars of creation" because they are filled with newborn stars.

Mars Up Close

Mars is Earth's neighbor in space. In the past, people studied Mars through telescopes. Now we can send probes to Mars to study the planet up close.

The red planet

Spinning around the sun are eight planets. The sun, its planets, and all other bodies that orbit the sun are called the **solar system.**

Earth is the third planet from the sun. Beyond Earth is Mars. When Earth and Mars come the closest to each other, they are about 34 ½ million miles (55.5 million kilometers) apart.

Mars has been called "the red planet" because its soils and rocks, rich in iron, give the planet a reddish color. In the past, **astronomers** wondered whether there was life on Mars. Through their telescopes, they thought they could see a network of crisscrossing lines. Some speculated that these lines were canals or other features built by intelligent beings. The lines proved to be an illusion, but the idea of life on Mars did not disappear.

The first Mars probes

Soon after the start of the Space Age, scientists began planning flights to Mars. The first successful Mars **probe,** Mariner 4, was launched by NASA in 1964. Mariner 4 flew by Mars, taking pictures of a dusty, barren world.

In 1971, Mariner 9 went into orbit around Mars and photographed most of the planet's surface. Mariner 9's images showed that Mars has canyons, volcanoes, and what appear to be dry riverbeds.

On July 20, 1976, the Viking 1 lander (lower right corner) captured the first photograph taken on the surface of Mars.

Photographs taken by the first successful Mars probe, Mariner 4, revealed a dusty, barren planet inhospitable to life.

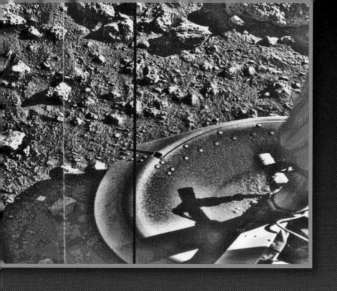

The surface of Mars was sampled for signs of life by the Viking 2 lander in 1976.

On the ground

The data returned to Earth by Mariner was fascinating, but it left many unanswered questions. NASA scientists and **engineers** planned a new Mars mission that would land on the planet's surface. The mission, called Viking, involved two spacecraft that would orbit Mars and send a landing vehicle to a different part of the planet's surface.

In August and September 1975, rockets blasted off from Earth carrying the Viking 1 orbiters. On July 20, 1976, the first of the orbiters set down its lander on Mars's surface. The second did the same on September 3.

Sights from a new world

The landers sent back pictures of the alien Martian world. They showed sandy, rocky ground and pink skies. The landers also returned the first weather readings from Mars. They confirmed that the Martian **atmosphere** was only about $1/100$ as dense as Earth's. They also reported temperatures far below the freezing point.

Scientists harvested an incredible amount of data from the Viking probes. As it turned out, there would be no more Earth visitors to Mars for another 20 years.

An image of the crater-scarred surface of Mars captured by Mariner 4 on July 15, 1965.

A very active period of Mars exploration began in 1996. Since then, space agencies have sent many probes to the planet.

By the mid-1990's, it had been 20 years since scientists had sent a **probe** to Mars. It was time to return. In 1996, NASA launched the Mars Pathfinder and the Mars Global Surveyor. Pathfinder landed on Mars in July 1997 and demonstrated new landing techniques. It also carried a Mars **rover** named Sojourner. Pathfinder sent spectacular photos back to Earth, and Sojourner analyzed soil and rocks. The Global Surveyor analyzed the planet from orbit.

Mars

Closer than ever

In August 2003, Mars passed closer to Earth than it had come in 60,000 years. Earth scientists launched three probes. The European Space Agency (ESA) launched Mars Express, another Mars orbiter. NASA sent two rovers, Spirit and Opportunity, to explore different parts of the Martian surface. The rovers landed on Mars in January 2004. They were designed for 90-day missions but continued to explore Martian ground for years.

NASA also launched the Mars Reconnaissance Orbiter in 2005 and the Phoenix lander in 2007.

An artist's rendering of one of the rovers exploring the Martian surface.

Dry—or wet?

Our exploration of Mars is just beginning. However, we have already learned a great deal about our neighbor in space.

Our earliest space probes seemed to show a desert planet with constant dust storms. However, later probes found large deposits of water-ice on Mars. In fact, the ESA's Mars Express discovered so much ice at the Martian south pole that it would, if melted, flood the planet with 36 feet (11 meters) of water.

Mars probes have found evidence that liquid water once gushed across the surface of Mars. They have found minerals usually formed in water on Earth. And they have photographed gullies and channels that seem to have been formed by rushing water. Scientists think that these features are very old.

Is there life on Mars?

As of now, there is no direct evidence of life on Mars. Most scientists agree that living things need liquid water to survive. Some scientists think life may have existed on Mars when it was warmer and wetter. There may even be pockets of liquid water underground where life could survive. Scientists will keep looking for life on Mars.

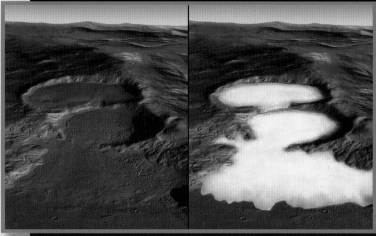

Rocky debris in craters on Mars (left) hides large underground glaciers (above right) in an artist's depiction. The depiction is based on data gathered by the Mars Reconnaissance Orbiter in 2008.

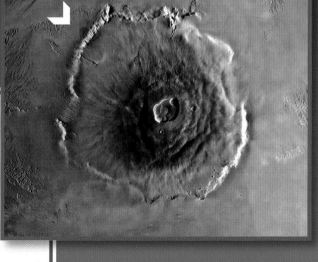

Olympus Mons

Did You Know?

Olympus Mons is the highest mountain on Mars. In fact, it is the tallest mountain in the **solar system**. It is about three times as high as Earth's tallest mountain, Mount Everest. Olympus Mons rises about 16 miles (26 kilometers) above the Martian surface.

Mercury and Venus Up Close

Mercury and Venus are the two planets closest to the sun. Several probes have visited these planets.

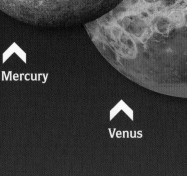

Mercury

Venus

Neighbors near the sun

Mercury is the planet closest to the sun. Venus is the next planet out from the sun. Venus is also closest to Earth. At its closest, Venus is about 23.7 million miles (38.2 million kilometers) from Earth. Space agencies have sent **probes** to both planets.

Mercury

NASA's Mariner 10 was the first space probe to visit Mercury. It flew by Mercury several times in 1974 and 1975. Mariner 10 confirmed that Mercury is a rocky, barren planet with almost no **atmosphere.** Like our moon, it is pockmarked with craters.

Because Mercury has almost no atmosphere, it is extremely hot during the day and bitterly cold at night. Its surface temperature ranges from 840 °F (450 °C) down to –275 °F (–170 °C).

Launched in 2004, the Messenger space probe flew past Mercury three times before entering into orbit around the planet in 2011. It photographed parts of the planet never seen before.

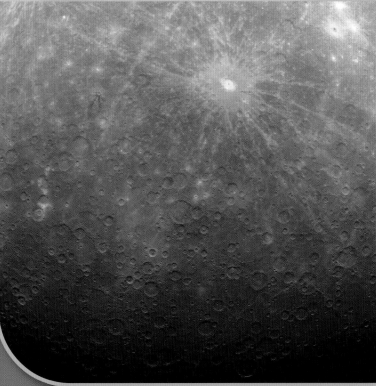

On March 29, 2011, Messenger captured its first image of Mercury as it orbited the planet.

At its closest approach, Venus is only about 99 times farther from Earth than the moon. It is not surprising that space agencies have sent a number of probes to Venus.

Venus is about the same size as Earth. People once thought that it might be similar to Earth. However, when probes began to visit Venus in the 1960's, they discovered that the planet is blanketed with an acid-filled atmosphere and that its surface bakes at about 870 °F (465 °C). Scientists now believe that Venus's dense atmosphere holds in more heat from the sun than it gives off. This is why the planet is like an oven.

Mariner 2, a NASA probe, flew by Venus in 1962. The first Soviet probe to Venus was Venera 2 in 1966. Both the United States and the Soviet Union continued to explore Venus with probes. In the late 1970's and early 1980's, U.S. and Soviet spacecraft sent small landing probes to the surface of Venus.

A NASA probe called Magellan orbited Venus from 1990 to 1994. Venus Express, a probe sent by the European Space Agency, began orbiting Venus in 2006.

Did You Know?

Venus has phases similar to those of the moon. We see phases of the moon here on Earth because only half of the sphere (ball) is sunlit. In some parts of its orbit, we see the moon's entire sunlit side. In other parts, we see only a sliver of this side. Phases of Venus appear for the same reasons. People on Earth need a telescope to see Venus's phases.

A color-enhanced mosaic of radar images taken by Magellan reveal the varied landscape of Venus.

Winged Feet

Astronomers of ancient Rome named the planet Mercury for Mercury, the messenger of the gods. In Roman myths, Mercury is sometimes described as having wings on his feet so he can run faster. The planet Mercury orbits the sun once every 88 days. From Earth, it seems to be moving faster than other heavenly bodies.

Jupiter, a giant planet, is the fifth planet from the sun. The first of several Earth probes reached Jupiter in 1979.

Giant Jupiter

Jupiter is the largest planet in the **solar system.** More than 1,000 Earths could fit inside Jupiter. Jupiter does not have a solid surface like Mercury, Venus, Earth, and Mars. It is sometimes called a gas giant because it is a huge sphere with a very thick outer layer of gases.

Pioneer 10 was the first Earth **probe** to reach Jupiter. It left Earth in March 1972 and flew by Jupiter in December 1973. Pioneer 10 and its twin, Pioneer 11—which reached Jupiter a year later—returned much data and many photos to Earth.

Meanwhile, NASA planned a broader mission to Jupiter and the other outer planets. It would include two probes, Voyager 1 and Voyager 2. NASA scientists called the planned trips of these probes "the Grand Tour."

The Grand Tour

Voyager 1 blasted off from Earth on September 5, 1977. It reached Jupiter in March 1979. Voyager 1 sent **astronomers** a big surprise: images of Jupiter with rings. The rings are so faint that Earth telescopes had never picked them up. The spacecraft also visited three of Jupiter's largest moons. Then Voyager 1 swung out from Jupiter and headed toward Saturn, the next planet in line.

Voyager 2 left Earth on August 20, 1977, and reached Jupiter in July 1979. The two Voyager spacecraft provided many new details about Jupiter's moons and also discovered new moons. Voyager 2, like its twin, headed next for Saturn.

Jupiter

Great Red Spot

Swirling clouds in Jupiter's Great Red Spot have been darkened in a false-color photograph to reveal detail.

Galileo

NASA designed the Galileo spacecraft to orbit Jupiter and study it over a period of time. Galileo was launched in 1989. It made a roundabout trip to Jupiter, arriving in December 1995. Galileo then went into orbit and stayed in orbit around Jupiter until 2003. Galileo also released a smaller probe that dropped into Jupiter's **atmosphere.** In all, the Galileo mission gained more information about Jupiter and its moons than all previous probes.

Jupiter's moons

Jupiter has four large moons and dozens of smaller ones. The Galileo probe gathered much data about the larger moons.

Io, a moon of Jupiter, is covered with active volcanoes. The volcanoes spew hot gases into space. Some of the gases freeze and fall back to Io's surface as colored snow.

The surface of Jupiter's moon Europa is a skin of ice. The ice looks cracked and refrozen, as if there is liquid water underneath. Many scientists think there is a huge ocean under this icy surface and that there could be life there.

Ganymede is not only Jupiter's largest moon but the largest moon in the solar system—larger even than Mercury. Ganymede is an icy world.

Callisto is Jupiter's second-largest moon. It is a dead world, heavily pocked by craters.

In February 2007, New Horizons passed close to Jupiter. The spacecraft is now halfway between Earth and Pluto. It is expected to fly past Pluto and its moons in July 2015.

A Hard Knock for Jupiter

In 1993, astronomers discovered a **comet** (small, icy body) passing near Jupiter. Astronomers soon realized that the comet, called Shoemaker-Levy 9, had been captured by Jupiter's gravity and broken into fragments. In July 1994, astronomers watched as some of the fragments crashed into Jupiter, creating dark regions in the gases surrounding the planet.

Jupiter's four large moons, in order of size: Ganymede, Callisto, Io, and Europa.

Saturn Up Close

Saturn is the sixth planet from the sun. The first of several Earth probes reached Saturn in 1979.

Saturn, like Jupiter, is a gas giant. Saturn is not as large as Jupiter—but it is many times larger than Earth. Whereas Jupiter's rings are so faint that they cannot be seen from Earth, Saturn's are wide and bright. Many people think Saturn is the most beautiful object in the **solar system.**

Probes to Saturn

NASA's Pioneer 11 was the first space **probe** to reach Saturn. After passing by Jupiter, Pioneer 11 flew within 13,000 miles (20,900 kilometers) of Saturn on September 1, 1979.

Saturn was the next stop after Jupiter on the Voyager's "Grand Tour." Voyager 1 reached Saturn in 1980. Voyager 2 reached the planet in 1981. The Voyager probes returned detailed photos of Saturn and several of its moons. The photos showed details of Saturn's rings never before seen.

Saturn has features that somewhat resemble storm systems on Earth. In 2004, the Dragon Storm, shown in a false-color photograph, generated lightning 10,000 times as strong as lightning on Earth.

Saturn's rings are made up of chunks of ice and rock. Some of the chunks are tiny. Others may be as big as a truck or even bigger.

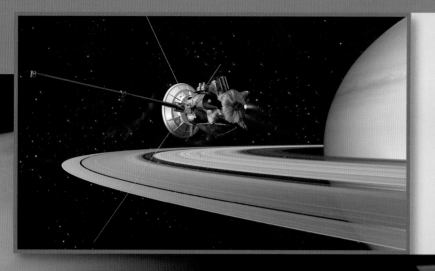

The Cassini probe was named for Giovanni Domenico Cassini (1625–1712), an Italian-born French **astronomer**. Cassini discovered four of Saturn's moons and described a gap in Saturn's ring system. The Huygens probe was named for Christiaan Huygens (1629–1695), a Dutch scientist who discovered Titan and contributed to the development of modern telescopes.

The Cassini probe

European space agencies cooperated with NASA to plan a special space mission to Saturn and its moons. The mission became known as the Cassini mission. The Cassini probe was launched from Earth in 1997. In July 2004, it went into orbit around Saturn.

Cassini sent back a wealth of data about Saturn and, of course, many detailed photos. It showed Saturn's huge ring system in greater detail than ever before. It also detected enormous thunderstorms and storms similar to hurricanes in Saturn's **atmosphere.**

Unmasking Titan

Saturn has more than 60 moons. The largest, Titan, has a dense atmosphere, unlike all other moons in the solar system. The atmosphere is mostly nitrogen. Titan also shows evidence of having seasons.

The Cassini probe carried a smaller probe, Huygens (*HOY gehns)*. In 2005, Cassini released Huygens, which landed on Titan's surface. It sent back thrilling images, including images of lakes and river systems that look much like those on Earth. However, they are filled with liquid ethane and methane. On Earth, these chemicals typically exist in the form of a gas. They become liquid only at very low temperatures. The Huygens probe reported atmospheric temperatures on Titan's surface of –290 °F (–178 °C).

One of Saturn's 60 moons, Titan, ranks as the second largest **satellite** in the solar system. It has lakes and river systems that look much like those on Earth but are filled with liquid ethane and methane. ⌄

The Outer Planets Up Close

Uranus is the seventh planet and Neptune is the eighth planet from the sun. The first probe reached Uranus in 1986 and Neptune in 1989.

Uranus

Uranus is a giant ball of gas and liquid. It is smaller than Jupiter and Saturn but about four times as wide as Earth.

Scientists learned much about Uranus in 1986. In January of that year, Voyager 2 flew within about 50,000 miles (80,000 kilometers) of the planet's cloudtops.

Uranus has faint rings. But the rings of Uranus do not extend from side to side like those of Saturn. Instead, they extend from top to bottom. That is because the axis (the imaginary line running through the middle of a planet, around which it spins) of Uranus lies almost on its side. Most other planets have an axis that is straight up and down or only slightly tilted.

Moons

Before the visit of Voyager 2 in 1986, **astronomers** knew only of five moons around Uranus. Today, we know of more than 25 moons around the planet.

Uranus

Miranda, a moon of Uranus

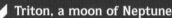
Neptune

Triton, a moon of Neptune

What's in a Name?

The planet Neptune was named for the Roman god of the sea. Neptune's swirling clouds are deep blue in color. The discoverers of Neptune thought that the blue color suggested water, or the sea.

In ancient myths of the Greeks, Triton was a son of Poseidon. Poseidon is the Greek version of Neptune—that is, the god of the sea. So Triton, the moon, is like a "son" to Neptune, the planet.

Neptune

Neptune is the farthest planet from the sun. It is about 30 times as far from the sun as Earth. It takes light 4 hours and 10 minutes to travel from the sun to Neptune.

Like Jupiter, Saturn, and Uranus, Neptune is a gas giant. It is nearly the same size as Uranus.

Little was known about Neptune until August 1989, when Voyager 2 flew by the planet. Voyager 2 discovered faint rings around Neptune and six moons not previously seen. Voyager sent back photos of Neptune showing its beautiful deep blue color.

Triton

Neptune has at least 13 moons. Its largest moon, Triton, is almost as large as Earth's own moon. Triton has a thin **atmosphere** made up mainly of nitrogen gas.

Triton is one of the coldest known bodies in the **solar system.** It has a surface temperature of about –390 °F (–235 °C).

In the 1990's and the 2000's, NASA and other space agencies sponsored new moon missions. However, no astronauts have visited the moon since 1972.

LCROSS was one of four missions to find evidence of water on the moon.

Between 1972 and 1994, there were no visits by astronauts or **probes** to the moon. But in January 1994, NASA sent the moon orbiter Clementine to the moon. From February to May of that year, Clementine took more than 2 million pictures of the moon. The orbiting probe also bounced laser beams and radar signals off the moon to examine its surface from orbit. The radar signals indicated large deposits of ice in craters around the moon's south pole.

More moon probes

In 1998 and 1999, NASA's Lunar Prospector probe orbited the moon and obtained more data. The Lunar Prospector gained new information about the chemical makeup of the moon and the magnetic field that surrounds the moon. It found strong evidence of ice at both the moon's north and south poles.

The European Space Agency got into the moon business, too. Its SMART-1 spacecraft orbited the moon from 2004 to 2006. SMART-1 added to our knowledge about the chemical makeup of the moon and other information about Earth's nearest neighbor.

Nations in Space

As of 2011, a number of nations, in addition to Russia and the United States, have developed space programs. Among them are China, the European Union member states, India, Iran, Israel, and Japan.

The pace quickens

After 2005, a number of nations sent probes to the moon. With every mission, we expand our knowledge of Earth's natural **satellite.** Now, more than 50 years after the start of the Space Age, we have mapped almost the entire surface of the moon.

Japan's space agency sent a spacecraft named Kayuga to the moon in 2007. It stayed in moon orbit for two years. Kayuga searched for water ice and minerals on the moon. At the same time, China launched its first moon probe. The spacecraft, named Chang'e 1, orbited the moon from 2007 to 2009.

India launched a moon probe in 2008. It was called Chandrayaan-1. The orbiting spacecraft mapped the moon's surface and released a smaller probe that landed on the moon.

In 2009, NASA sent two more missions to the moon. They were the Lunar Reconnaissance Orbiter (LRO) and the Lunar Crater Observation and Sensing Satellite (LCROSS). In November of that year, LCROSS confirmed the presence of water ice at the moon's south pole.

Boots on the moon?

Space scientists, **engineers,** and others are eager to send astronauts to the moon again. At present, no space agency has immediate plans for an Apollo-style moon mission. However, many people hope to see astronauts on the moon by 2020.

South Pole

Clementine Mission
Uncontrolled Image Mosaic
Lunar South Polar Region
Orthographic Projection

▲ A mosaic of images taken from the Clementine mission reveals the location of water (shown in blue) on the moon's south pole.

At the Same Time...

China's space program sent its first astronaut into space in October 2003. The astronaut, Yang Liwei, orbited Earth for 21 hours in a Chinese-made spacecraft and returned home safely.

▲ Yang Liwei

Comets and Asteroids Up Close

Comets and asteroids are bodies in the solar system that are smaller than planets and most moons. Scientists have studied these bodies with powerful telescopes and with spacecraft.

Comet McNaught, shown in the sky above the Pacific Ocean in 2007, may be the largest comet ever measured. Data collected by the space probe Ulyssess in 2007 indicate that McNaught's tail may trail the comet's nucleus for as much as 159 miles (256,000 kilometers).

Comets

A **comet** is an icy body that travels in an elliptical (oval-shaped) path around the sun and releases gas or dust as it nears the sun. A comet consists of a core called the nucleus and a long "tail" of gas and vapor that points away from the sun. The tail is most visible as the comet nears the sun.

Studying comets

Before the Space Age, scientists could study comets only with telescopes. Recently, space agencies have sent **probes** to comets.

In 1986, Halley's Comet passed near Earth. The European Space Agency sent the Giotto probe to study the comet. Giotto and several other space probes returned much data about Halley. The comet's nucleus is about 9 miles (15 kilometers) long and looks a bit like a potato. It is made up mainly of water ice and dust.

Other spacecraft have allowed scientists to learn even more about comets. In 2006, the space probe Stardust flew close enough to a comet to collect a sample. Stardust dropped the sample to Earth before continuing on to study another comet.

Did You Know?

Astronomers believe that comets are leftover debris from the formation of the outer planets. A collection of gas, ice, rocks, and dust formed the outer planets about 4.6 billion years ago. Some scientists believe that comets originally brought to Earth some of the water and the carbon-based molecules that make up living things.

Asteroids

An **asteroid** is a chunk of rock or metal that orbits the sun. A large number of asteroids exist in a belt between Mars and Jupiter.

Occasionally, collisions knock asteroids out of their normal orbits. A stray asteroid can strike Earth, though this happens only rarely. However, an impact by a large asteroid can cause severe damage. Scientists believe this happened 65 million years ago and caused the extinction of dinosaurs.

Today, scientists are watching for stray asteroids that could hit Earth. Most scientists believe that an asteroid on a collision course with Earth could be easily nudged into a different path by a planned collision with a spacecraft if spotted early enough.

Visits to asteroids

A number of space probes have visited asteroids. NASA's Galileo probe, designed to visit Jupiter, studied several asteroids on its way to the giant planet. Galileo visited an asteroid named Ida in 1993 and made a surprising discovery. Tiny Ida has its own moon. Since 1993, scientists have discovered other asteroids with moons.

In 1996, NASA launched the Near-Earth Asteroid Rendezvous (NEAR) spacecraft. In 2001, NEAR became the first space-craft to land on an asteroid.

Japan launched the Hayabusa probe to study asteroids. In 2005, it landed on the asteroid Itokawa and returned a sample of the asteroid to Earth in 2010.

The asteroid Itokawa appears to consist of two physically distinct pieces loosely held together by gravity.

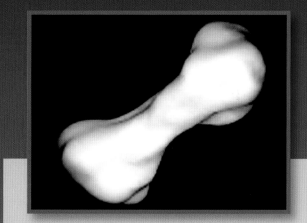

A Rock for Fido

Asteroids come in all shapes and sizes. In the main asteroid belt between Mars and Jupiter, astronomers discovered a most unusual asteroid they named Kleopatra. It is shaped like a dog-bone treat. Kleopatra is about 135 miles (217 kilometers) long and 58 miles (94 kilometers) wide.

Astronomers hope that space exploration may one day reach far beyond the solar system. But no one knows if traveling such a great distance is even possible.

Over the past half-century, human beings have explored the moon, planets, **comets, asteroids,** and other parts of the **solar system.** The next barrier to be broken is the edge of the solar system. We long to travel to other stars, planetary systems, and **galaxies.** And that won't be easy.

Obstacles to distant space travel

Voyages to the edge of the solar system would have to cover almost unimaginable distances. To make any progress at all, a spaceship would have to travel at or near the speed of light. That alone poses many problems.

No spacecraft known to us can travel at such a speed. But even if it could, there is another problem. According to Albert Einstein, a great scientist of the 1900's, time itself would slow down as you approach the speed of light. That means that astronauts traveling to a distant star or planet would stay relatively young while their friends and family back on Earth aged and perhaps died.

There are many problems to be worked out if human beings are ever to travel across interstellar space (space between the stars). In fact, such travel may prove impractical or even impossible. Of course, these challenges won't stop people from trying.

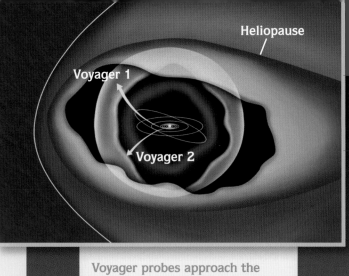

Voyager probes approach the heliopause in an artist's diagram.

Albert Einstein 〉

The Voyager interstellar mission

In 1977, NASA launched the planetary **probes** Voyager 1 and Voyager 2 to study the outer planets. The Voyager probes flew past Neptune in 1989—and they are still going.

Scientists hope to learn about space beyond the solar system in a few years. They believe that the Voyager spacecraft have enough fuel to keep going until at least 2020.

As of 2011, Voyager 1, the farthest probe, was approaching the heliopause, the boundary between the solar system and interstellar space. At that time the probe was about 10.8 billion miles (17.4 billion kilometers) out from the sun.

The Kepler mission

In March 2009, NASA launched the Kepler probe. The probe is designed to look for planets around stars in a section of the Milky Way galaxy. It is equipped with very sensitive instruments to measure light. The instruments can detect the faint flicker that occurs when a planet passes in front of a star and blocks some of its light. Kepler is orbiting the sun in the same path as Earth, but it trails Earth.

Most of the planets that Kepler has detected are gas giants similar to Jupiter. But scientists hope to find some Earthlike planets. Such planets would have about the same mass and volume as Earth and would lie at about the same distance from their stars.

Ideas that Shook the World

Albert Einstein (1879–1955) developed entirely new scientific ideas that related space to time. He also explained how energy and matter are related. Many people consider Einstein one of the greatest scientists of all time.

What's in a Name?

The Kepler space probe is named for Johannes Kepler (1571–1630). Kepler, a German scientist, developed theories of planetary motion that explained how Earth and the other planets orbit the sun. Kepler was not the first scientist to claim that Earth orbits the sun, rather than the sun orbiting Earth. But he was the first to work out this idea mathematically.

An artist's rendering of the Kepler probe. >

What will space exploration be like 50 or 100 years from now? We cannot answer this question—but we can make some educated guesses about our future in space.

Virgin Galactic's VSS *Enterprise* flies above the site of Virgin's unfinished spaceport in New Mexico.

Private companies in space

One of the most interesting trends in recent years has been the activities of private companies in space. Some companies have begun developing their own rockets, spacecraft, and **satellites.**

In December 2010, the SpaceX Company of Hawthorne, California, launched its own **space capsule** on a rocket. Ships picked up the capsule in the Pacific Ocean after it returned to Earth.

Another company, Virgin Galactic, developed new spacecraft in the early 2000's. The company offered rides into space on its spacecraft—for a hefty ticket fee. Some experts predicted that, in time, people might book flights on spaceships just as they now do on jets.

Space stations

The success of the ISS suggests that space stations will be an important part of our future in space. Space scientists and **engineers** are designing bigger space stations that will provide greater comfort and safety for astronauts.

The next generation of space station is likely to include facilities to service spacecraft. Spacecraft in Earth's orbit could stop at a space service station to fuel up or at a repair shop to have problems fixed. This kind of service could make space travel safer.

World's First Spaceport

In the 2000's, Virgin Galactic and other companies began building the world's first commercial spaceport. The ultramodern facility is in the desert in southwestern New Mexico.

Colonizing the moon

Some space experts are working on plans to set up stations on the moon. A moon station could serve as a jumping-off point for further space travel. Some stations could be built to function as mining camps. Scientists believe that the moon contains many valuable minerals.

Providing support systems for astronauts stationed on the moon would pose a big challenge. However, scientists now know that the moon has large ice deposits near its poles. The ice could provide a ready supply of water to moon stations.

Colonizing Mars

Many science experts believe that people will travel to Mars sometime in the next 25 years. Once Earth has established an outpost on Mars, the red planet may tempt us to come back again and again.

Some scientists have suggested that people could "terraform" Mars—that is, make changes over time that would make the planet livable to Earth's people, plants, and animals. Is this idea possible? No one knows for sure.

The future?

What is certain about our future in space is that human curiosity will continue to drive us on. Like our ancestors, those who come after us will surely desire to push beyond our familiar world into unknown worlds.

▲ Humans may one day establish colonies on Mars to explore the planet over long periods.

"Journey" to Mars

In June 2010, six astronauts started a journey to Mars. But the journey was simulated (pretend). The astronauts entered a space facility in Moscow, Russia, and prepared to live inside a spacecraft for 520 days, cut off from the world. That's how long scientists believe a Mars mission with astronauts would take. The estimate includes time to spend a month on Mars.

artificial satellite a human-made object that continuously orbits Earth or some other body in space.

asteroid a chunk of rock or metal that orbits the sun.

astronomer a scientist who studies the heavens.

atmosphere the blanket of air surrounding Earth.

comet an icy body that travels in an oblong path around the sun and releases gas or dust as it nears the sun. The gas and dust form the comet's "tail."

cosmonaut an astronaut, especially a Russian astronaut.

engineer a person who plans and builds engines, machines, roads, bridges, canals, or the like.

galaxy a vast system of stars, gas, dust, and other matter held together in space by their mutual gravitational pull.

microgravity the condition of having so little gravity that objects are almost weightless.

module a section that can function either by itself or with other parts.

payload the top part of a rocket that contains the cargo—perhaps including human passengers.

probe a spacecraft that carries scientific instruments but no people.

rocketry the science of making and using rockets.

rover a small, skatelike vehicle that can roll along the ground and perform various tests. Rovers have been used on Mars.

satellite an object in space that revolves around a planet, especially around one of the planets of the solar system. Also see *artificial satellite.*

solar panel a flat, thin surface containing thousands of solar cells— tiny devices that harvest energy from sun rays to produce electricity.

solar system the sun, its planets, and all other bodies that orbit the sun.

space capsule a type of payload that becomes its own spacecraft when separated from a rocket.

Books

The Adventures of Sojourner: The Mission to Mars that Thrilled the World by Susi Trautmann Wunsch (Mikaya Press, 1998)

Astronauts: Life Exploring Outer Space by Chris Hayhurst (Rosen Publishing Group, 2001)

Can You Hear a Shout in Space?: Questions and Answers About Space Exploration by Melvin Berger and others (Scholastic Reference, 2000)

Close Encounters: Exploring the Universe with the Hubble Space Telescope by Elaine Scott (Hyperion Books for Children, 1998)

Disasters in Space Exploration by Gregory Vogt (Millbrook Press, 2001)

Escape from Earth by Peter Ackroyd (DK Publishing, 2003)

Exploring the Solar System: A History with 22 Activities by Mary Kay Carson (Chicago Review Press, 2006)

Galileo Spacecraft: Mission to Jupiter by Michael D. Cole (Enslow Publishers, 1999)

Mission Control, This Is Apollo: The Story of the First Voyages to the Moon by Andrew Chaikin and Victoria Kohl (Viking, 2009)

Small Worlds: Exploring the 60 Moons of Our Solar System by Joseph W. Kelch (J. Messner, 1990)

Women in Space by Carol S. Briggs (Lerner Publications, 1998)

Websites

Amazing Space
http://amazing-space.stsci.edu/

Learn more about astronomy and the science behind space exploration at this educational website from the Space Telescope Science Institute. Includes a homework help section.

Apollo to the Moon
http://www.nasm.si.edu/exhibitions/attm/enter.html

This online exhibition from the National Air and Space Museum uses images, artifacts, and primary source documents to tell the story of the Apollo missions.

Hubble Site
http://hubblesite.org/

Learn more about the Hubble Space Telescope, its observations and discoveries, and its successor—the James Webb Space Telescope. Featuring video podcasts about new developments.

Kids Astronomy
http://www.kidsastronomy.com/

At this website, you can explore deep space, track the phases of the moon, and map the positions of the stars.

Mission: The International Space Station
http://www.nasa.gov/mission_pages/station/main/index.html

Learn about life and work aboard the International Space Station at this website, which also features fun and educational videos and slideshows.

NASA Kids' Club
http://www.nasa.gov/audience/forkids/kidsclub/flash/index.html

At this educational website, you can read about NASA's latest missions and meet the scientists and astronauts who are working to explore our solar system.

Windows to the Universe
http://www.windows2universe.org/

This site from the National Earth Science Teachers Association covers such topics as the solar system, constellations, space mythology, and more.

Women at NASA
http://www.nasa.gov/vision/space/preparingtravel/women_at_nasa.html

Meet the inspirational women who work in all fields at NASA, from the engineers and scientists on the ground to the astronauts who have gone into space.